A Simple Guide To Train Your Dog

Use Clicker Training to Teach Your Dog to Walk on a Leash, Sit, Stay, Go to Potty and Obey Your Commands

By Smart Reads

Free Audiobook

As a thank you for being a Smart Reader you can choose 2 FREE audiobooks from audible.com. Simply sign up for free by visiting www.audibletrial.com/Travis to get your books.

Visit:
www.smartreads.co/freebooks
to receive Smart Reads books for FREE

Check us out on Instagram:
www.instagram.com/smart_readers
@smart_readers

ABOUT SMARTREADS

Choose Smart Reads and get smart every time. Smart Reads sorts through all the best content and condenses the most helpful information into easily digestible chunks.

We design our books to be short, easy to read and highly informative. Leaving you with maximum understanding in the least amount of time.

Smart Reads aims to accelerate the spread of quality information so we've taken the copyright off everything we publish and donate our material directly to the public domain. You can read our uncopyright below.

We believe in paying it forward and donate 5% of our net sales to Pencils of Promise to build schools, train teachers and support child education.

To limit our footprint and restore forests around the globe we are planting a tree for every 10 hardcover books we sell.

Thanks for choosing Smart Reads and helping us help the planet.

Sincerely,

Travis & the Smart Reads Team

Uncopyright 2017 by Smart Reads. No rights reserved worldwide. Any part of this publication may be reproduced or transmitted in any form without the prior written consent of the publisher.

Disclaimer: The publisher and author make no representations or warranties with respect to the accuracy or completeness of these contents and disclaim all warranties for a particular purpose. The author or publisher is not responsible for how you use this information. The fact that an individual or organization is referred to in this document as a citation or source of information does not imply that the author or publisher endorses the information that the individual or organization provided.

TABLE OF CONTENTS

Introduction 2

Chapter 1: Obedience Training 3

Chapter 2: Barking In the Car 6

Chapter 3: Curbing Territorial Aggression 9

Chapter 4: Clicker Training - the Basics 12

Chapter 5: Respecting the Yard 24

Chapter 6: How to Stop Detrimental Chewing 38

Chapter 7: Providing Guidance to Your Dog 43

Conclusion 51

Smart Reads Vision 54

INTRODUCTION

Training your dog properly is something every dog owner must do. Those who love dogs want to have and maintain a loving, long-lasting, relationship with their pets. Training will provide the basic foundation for this kind of relationship. More than just promoting a good relationship, the right training is vital for maintaining safety for the dog and the family.

The training process isn't a quick one-day affair but rather something that will require love, dedication and patience from you. If you invest the right amount of time and the effort to train your dog properly it will be much easier than having to retrain and correct any bad behaviors in the future.

Keep the end goal in mind when you first start training a dog. Think about the pride you'll feel after your pooch has been transformed from an unruly puppy to a disciplined, well-behaved dog, the kind you've dreamed of.

CHAPTER 1: OBEDIENCE TRAINING

In order to fully understand the process of obedience training, you must first re-learn or re-think the way you view it. It is similar to other types of education in that it requires reassurance and patience. Dogs are intelligent animals and they like to learn different and new things. They find this rewarding. They also experience frustration just like humans do when they don't perform well. In reality, training dogs is similar to sending children to kindergarten.

One thing you must remember is that you mustn't have any unrealistic expectations regarding your pet's early training. Way before a dog can learn to sit, stay, and fetch, for example, it has to first learn how to learn. For most dogs, just being placed in a group of other, unfamiliar dogs is an overwhelming experience. The dogs must learn how to socialize and this is a big step.

Each of us will most likely have similar goals for our dog's training but we will also have some different ones as well. Some will want their dog to perform tricks and obey commands, others will be happy as long as their dog behaves well when in public, doesn't chew the furniture, and is toilet trained. Generally speaking, you will find that once your pet starts the learning process, he/she will likely pick up new things a lot faster as time goes on. You might even find it exciting to train your dog.

There are certain commands that every dog must learn so that he/she can be well-behaved in public. There are 5 commands that are absolutely necessary and these are: Come, Sit, Stay, Down, and Heel. Most of the obedience programs will consider dogs to be well trained if they can follow these five commands each time their owner gives them.

A well-trained dog is a lot more fun and generally more pleasant and easy to live with.

Most of us know a dog that runs amok inside the house, doesn't follow any commands, and generally makes life hard for everyone. These types of dogs are disobedient. Sometimes they are dangerous as well. Taking any dog that doesn't follow orders or won't stay or heel in a park when off-the-leash can put itself, other dogs and even other people, at risk. Knowing only a few simple commands will make dogs more capable and more obedient.

For some of you, advancing the education of your dog might be something you want. If this is the case, think of the training as furthering his/her education, just the same as you would a child. Your dog will learn to do other things, those that do not come to him/her naturally. The dog will not find the newer commands so intuitive and then it will probably take more effort on the dog's part in order for him/her to succeed. Your patience and your positive reinforcement will help with this process.

The AKC (American Kennel Club) maintains a guide to the obedience level training achieved. This system of training is done in trials, and then into grades or classes. The advancement through the grades is similar to kids moving through school all the way up.

CHAPTER 2: BARKING IN THE CAR

There are so many distractions while driving a car, especially today with all the modern gadgets, GPS systems, and of course, sound systems. Not only do you have to deal with these distractions but you also have to keep your eyes firmly on the road and watch and anticipate other drivers as well.

For those with a dog, an added distraction is in the car. This is especially the case if your dog is the kind who barks a lot while in the car. He/she might see another dog, a cat, someone on a bike etc. and will bark at every one of them, and on it goes. This can cause a lot of stress for many people and it can become a bit too much. Some people might start yelling at the dog and bring even more stress to an already stressful situation because the dog will likely become more agitated. Perhaps it might even believe they are joining it as it barks at everything it sees and thinks it is doing something good.

As mentioned, a well-trained dog makes a good pet and part of the training will include the dog knowing when to bark and when to keep quiet. A dog that barks non-stop will be annoying and any responsible dog owner must be able to easily silence his/her pet.

Below are Some Ideas on How To Do This:
1. Dogs take their cues from their masters. If the master is loud, the dog will also be loud. If the master is calm and not stressed then the dog will also be calmer, following their lead. Petting the dog gently and speaking to it softly will tell the dog that he/she can relax and be at ease. Dogs want your attention so when you give it to them without them being noisy they will learn everything is okay.

2. For some dogs, however, they may need more persuasion. In some cases, dog owners train the dogs to stop what they're doing if the owner squirts water at them, for example. A little spritz is usually enough to calm a dog that is barking and it will not harm the dog or the car's interior. Most dogs, do not like being squirted with water, especially puppies, and they will stop doing whatever they're doing when the owner does this. Remember that speaking to your pet dog softly after you spray it is important. Gently pet the dog if you can so it knows it has been rewarded for behaving well.

3. For some dogs, none of the above ideas will work. There are some dogs that need to be transported in crates to remain calm. It's a good idea to keep the crate below the window level so the dog cannot see any distractions. This may not be something you can

do with a big dog but for others, consistently using a crate to transport your dog will let him/her know that it's time to keep quiet. Talk to your dog using a mild, soft voice as this will reassure your pet. In this way you will both get what you want.

CHAPTER 3: CURBING TERRITORIAL AGGRESSION

Even though dogs have been domesticated now for centuries, they might still display aggressiveness. Many dog owners strive to ensure their dogs are trained well enough so they are calm and even-tempered. However, there still exist some inherent traits in every dog that might be displayed using aggression.

"Territorial aggression" is a term used to describe behavior that is most commonly displayed by dogs. This is when dogs bark or become overly protective any time a stranger comes near the home.

So what triggers this aggression in some dogs? As already mentioned, dogs become aggressive when they are protecting their belongings or their home and this is actually a natural response from a dog. However, there are also other situations that can trigger this kind of response in a dog. Some of them are mentioned below:

1. When a dog's aggression is reinforced. Something simple such as a person coming by your house when you're not there could do it. The individual will knock or ring the bell. The dog will bark furiously and the

person will leave. Of course, the person is leaving because no one has answered the door but the dog thinks the individual is leaving due to the dog's protective barking and aggression. So, the dog interprets this to mean that he/she has driven the person away and successfully protected their area or their territory.

2. When a dog travels in the car with you and constantly barks at the passing vehicles and people. The dog is essentially telling everybody to keep away from his or her territory, in this case, the vehicle. This provides the positive reinforcement mentioned above because of course, when you are driving, people don't usually approach the car. The dog believes it is keeping the other people away so it thinks it has been successful in protecting the master's vehicle and so will keep on barking.

3. This scenario was briefly mentioned above - when a dog starts being aggressive and barking, for example, and his master screams so it can be quiet. In the dog's mind, his/her owner is also engaging in this aggressive behavior. This then reinforces the behavior of the dog rather than deterring it. Yelling at a dog when it's barking will likely encourage the dog and it will continue to bark.

4. Another situation, which might cause a dog to display aggressive type behavior, is if you lock it in another room of the house when you have company over. Perhaps you think that you're solving this problem but you're probably making the situation worse. Your dog can smell other people, the "intruders," but cannot do anything and feels helpless. This can lead to high anxiety levels for the dog and this can then translate into excessively aggressive behavior.

CHAPTER 4: CLICKER TRAINING – THE BASICS

We communicate with dogs using signals. We make these signals with our body, our voice, or hand gestures. Communication is actually the most effective and simple means of dog training. You have to find an effective type of communication that your dog will respond to. There are two key things that will ensure effective communication with your dog: being consistent and being precise.

An effective tool for doing this is a clicker device. Some people also use a whistle. Using a clicker to provide feedback is a good way to communicate to a dog that it has performed an action you wanted. Dogs will quickly begin to associate the clicker sound with getting a reward because they've done a good job and obeyed a command.

Many different clicker styles exist. You can buy then in many different shapes, sizes, and colors. Find one that will feel comfortable when it's in your hand. Make sure it's one you can press easily. Clickers are usually small and not expensive.

How Does the Clicker Training Work?

The clicker works when the dog starts associating the clicker sound with receiving a valued treat after it has properly responded to the master's command. You could use small pieces of cheese, flavored treats, chicken or whatever your dog really likes.

Dogs tend to favorably respond to food rewards as they are reinforced when they respond to the clicking sound, but there are also other types of rewards that dogs will respond to well. These include getting some playtime with you, some physical affection, or perhaps even getting a drink of cool water. The rewards you offer the dog will be associated with the clicker sound, so the reward is the primary reinforcer.

When you train your pet to associate certain rewards with a particular sound you are actually engaging in "classical conditioning." This is also known as Pavlovian conditioning, based on Ivan Pavlov's experiments with dogs. To the dog, the clicker sound becomes associated with a food reward and the clicking becomes the secondary reinforcer.

For the dog, the clicker sound is basically you saying "good dog" to your dog when it does as you have ordered. Let's say you're training the dog or puppy to sit. Anytime that you see the dog sit down, say the command "sit" then make a click and give the reward. The dog is smart enough to quickly associate doing the command with getting a treat.

The dog will want to continue pleasing you because the clicking sound corresponded with the dog performing as you wanted it to. Using a clicker can be more effective as a training tool instead of offering praise alone because most people are more consistent when clicking than they are in actually praising their pets.

Most people will praise their dogs during the day and so this praise will become less valuable to the dog in its mind. Not so with a clicking sound. Clicking is also much faster than saying the words "good boy/girl" so the dog gets instant gratification.
Using the clicker consistently along with a reward will see the dog obeying you much faster. You will be on the way to having a well-behaved, happy dog and you will feel proud of the success you have achieved as a dog trainer. This particular training strategy is easy and simple for both you and the dog.

Begin By Creating Positive Associations
A big benefit of clicker usage is that the dog will start associating positive results with particular actions.

What does it mean for a dog to associate a positive outcome with a certain action?

To give an example, if you happen to touch the dog food bag as you are moving something else, the dog will be at your side in no time wagging its tail and waiting for some food. This is because, over time, the dog has begun to associate the rustling of a bag with being fed. The same will also apply to other types of actions as well, like when you pick up the leash; the dog thinks it will go for a walk.

You can see the pattern and can understand that a dog trained in this manner will give you certain behavior, and listen to commands that he/she knows will be followed by a reward. Some examples are things like waiting patiently while food is put in their bowl, sitting while you attach their leash to the collar.

The situation will be this: your dog won't be able to wait to perform any command you give it because it knows a positive reward or treat will come after it. The clicker creates the same type of associations of a jingling leash or dog food bag. It makes the dog feel excited about training and it will pay attention carefully.

Bridging an Action with a Reward Using Your Clicker

The clicker is useful for dog training because it provides you with more time to reward the dog. It is always better to reward a dog quickly so the clicker is perfect for this. If you are across the yard and give the dog a certain command, there'll be a little delay between the time the dog performs and when they get the reward. The dog might start receiving mixed signals and may not be sure if he/she is doing what you want.

The clicker, however, will alert the dog instantly that he has done exactly as he was asked and then he will wait for his treat. This way there is no confusion. Your dog will start to understand exactly what he should do when he's given a particular command.

Giving Life Rewards for Good Behavior

As you know, a clicker is one way of teaching a dog new behavior. When your dog starts following commands immediately, there will be no need to continue using the clicker. You can begin rewarding the dog with affection. This can come in the form of praise, or some physical contact like petting the dog. Something else that you can use as a reward for your dog is a life reward.

These life rewards consist of something other than food, things that your dog wants. For example, you might tell your dog "sit" and when the dog does it you could take him/her for a walk.

Fun and Games with Clicker Training
Using a clicker for training is mostly associated with puppy training and for more basic commands such as "sit" or "stay." A training professional knows that the clicker training is good for training more behaviors which can lead to happier relationships for the dogs and the owners.

Kevin Alexander, a specialist in clicker training, explains it like this: Puppies quickly understand that a clicking sound actually means something good. It knows it did something that made the click happen. Alexander often trains pups as young as three weeks old. One time he even trained a group of retriever puppies to lift up their paws on command. This only took him a few minutes.

Clicker training strategies are useful for teaching many types of behaviors. Kevin Alexander utilizes the clicker for teaching complicated behaviors, like standing still when asked to, or going and standing at the door if he/she needs to go outside. These behaviors are more complicated and must be developed in stages by training the one part and then the other to add to the first behavior.

It is possible to form more complex behaviors from simpler ones like raising one paw. A trainer will start by encouraging a dog to raise its paw with just a click. After that, the trainer might decide to add something like a "high five" to this behavior and further reinforce this. The behavior could then develop into something else like perhaps ringing a small bell. It is the clicker that will take something that seems impossible for a puppy and teach him/her in a manner that is gradual. Eventually the puppy will understand that you want a specific thing from it and it will start to do it on its own. The puppy will understand that a bigger world exists around it and it can actually interact with this world. Kevin Alexander says that it is fun seeing a puppy begin to make this particular realization.

One thing you must know is that not every dog is prone to obedience. Dogs like terriers or tracking dogs tend to be like this. Typically, these types of dogs do not have much ambition for gaining their owners approval like many other breeds do. The clicker will come in particularly handy with these breeds. Instead of behaving in a certain way to get affection from their masters, the click will give them motivation to perform tricks and believe it was actually their idea.

Clicker training is effective with pretty much every breed of dog; however, it is particularly effective for use with dog breeds that are somewhat indifferent to obedience training. It is best to start clicker training when the puppy is quite young, about 3 weeks old. Remember to be patient with the little ones as they are young.

More Fun with the Clicker
Using a clicker to train your dog is simple and it's fast. It is a great way to teach a puppy some useful behaviors such as polite manners, neat tricks, or fun commands instead of obedience commands.

Puppies will catch on quickly to this type of training and the process is simple. Firstly, load the clicker and charge it, and then start to familiarize yourself with it. Puppies will usually associate a clicker with treats. The puppy will focus on your clicker first, before it figures out that it is his own behavior that's actually generating the click. An expert clicker can get a puppy to concentrate on a clicker for about 10 minutes at a time.

Peaceful Greetings
A really good training method, and one which many trainers like, is the peaceful greetings method. It

teaches dogs that "no jumping" can actually be rewarding and fun. It is a way of training puppies that are usually excitable and greet a visitor by running over and jumping on them again and again. Of course, this is the puppy showing how friendly and enthusiastic it is but it's recommended that a puppy be trained so it is more restrained in its greeting behavior and will receive a reward every time it greets someone peacefully. This is better taught in groups or perhaps with a partner.

This is how to train your dog to peacefully greet people:

1. Your partner should hold the leash as well as the clicker and you should be standing further away with some treats.

2. Approach your puppy and wait to see if he/she will jump on you. If the puppy jumps, don't make any eye contact and don't speak any commands. Repeat the first step - approach and then back up again.

3. Once this is done a few times, your puppy will realize it will have to alter its own behavior. It will start keeping its little paws firmly on the ground when you begin approaching. When this occurs, the partner

who is holding onto the leash should click and then you reward the pup with praise and a treat.

4. You should continue with this strategy until your puppy does this without having to be on a leash. At this point your pup has learnt what to do and what not to do.

5. A really good training method involves children who call to the puppy. When a child calls and the puppy comes, it should be ignored if it starts to jump up, but if it behaves and doesn't jump it should be given praise and a treat with the click. A puppy can usually be completely trained in only 1 or 2 sessions.

Going to the Mat
A common game that many people play with their dogs is called "to the mat." It requires the puppy go to its little mat then lie down when you ask it to. You might think that active puppies won't do this but it can easily be taught. It is a game but it also has other uses. For example, it can be used for enticing a puppy into the car, away from other people, or anywhere you might want it to go.

You can use the clicker again to train the puppy. You can show your puppy that just hanging around on its mat can actually be enjoyable. First, we want this to be an easy exercise and not a difficult one so place the puppy mat in front of your puppy. If the mat is far away it will be more difficult. Make sure you are ready to use the clicker straight away because your puppy will likely investigate and sniff the mat before you give any command. Give the puppy a nice treat when it starts to sniff the mat.

Once the puppy has sniffed and investigated it will naturally wonder what will come next. If your puppy leaves its mat and comes over to you, you should not do anything, but if lies on its mat, use your clicker then give your dog a treat. Whenever your puppy does something that includes the mat and is seen as a positive type of action, it should get a reward.

You can make this process gradual, so be prepared to use the clicker as each step is achieved. Move the puppy mat further away slowly so as to encourage it to walk to the mat using clicks and treats. Ignore it if it moves further from its mat. You can always use treats to encourage the puppy to step closer to its mat. If it walks to the mat after seeing the treat, use your clicker to show your approval. The point is to make your puppy understand that what you want is its paws on the mat. Always remember to have patience with your little pup as this may take several practice sessions.

Once your puppy is on its mat standing, use your clicker and encourage your puppy to either sit or to lie on it.

When you are training your puppy to do this, verbal commands must be included as well. Tell the puppy to "go to the mat" or to "sit on the mat." In this way, your dog will associate the word mat with its mat. It will then go there without you having to use the clicker or any treats when the pup gets older.

CHAPTER 5: RESPECTING THE YARD

Having a back yard will make owning a dog easier. You can begin training it for outdoor potty right away. A back yard is the perfect place for young, energetic puppies to explore safely and the owner doesn't have to supervise it constantly.
It isn't a good idea though, to use your back yard as a place for keeping the dog when guests come over or as a place to run around because you don't have time to take it for a nice walk.

Without proper supervision, a dog could start to think independently and you might find that later on, your dog doesn't really obey your commands, as it should. This can be difficult to reverse. So, make sure you properly train your dog from the beginning.

It is a fact that dogs are social animals. They prefer company to being alone, and that company is their owners, preferably and other animals. A dog can easily start to feel lonely and it can become bored leading it to get into all sorts of mischief. Perhaps you might come home to find your garden full of holes, or your garden hose chewed up. Trying to figure out a way to get into the neighbor's back yard could become important to your dog. In some cases, a dog will start barking excessively if it hears other dogs in the neighborhood.

A dog that is sufficiently supervised will not likely learn these bad habits. This is because you will be present to redirect it and ensure it engages in another preferred activity like say, playing fetch the ball or learning about the appropriate place to go potty. The younger dogs in particular need this type of constant training and interaction in order for them to grow up and become the type of adult dog you want them to be. A dog needs to learn what you like and what you don't like regarding pretty much everything. It is important to understand that obedience training isn't a skill learned in isolation. You must put in all the work because you are actually the most essential and important factor in this situation.

When a dog displays good behavior, try and rewarded it immediately. When it displays poor behaviors just redirect your dog. Rewards will increase the probability of your dog adopting a new behavior. After all, it is praise and treats that are wonderful for your pet.

Your backyard is the perfect place for your dog to get some exercise and also blow off some energy. However, dogs need human interaction and they need it from their masters. This is something you must provide. Dogs need to learn about how they can build some positive, constructive relationships with the people around them. They need to bond. This will be impossible if a dog doesn't get his/her one-on-one special time with its human.

Having a proper plan for ensuring a dog, especially a young one, gets enough interaction and exercise is vital. If you are not home most of the time due to work commitments etc. think about getting a good dog walker to help that time get filled in for your dog. Another option is doggie daycare. Look them up in your local area. In addition, you could consider making a doggy door or even a dog proof area inside your home. These can be quite useful strategies. Try out some of these ideas until you are sure that your dog can be okay when left alone in the house.

Digging
If you find that your backyard is full of craters because your dog is continually digging, there could be numerous reasons for this. Perhaps it's been hunting for little critters or some buried treasure that it can smell. Perhaps it needed a cool area to sit or lie in on a hot day. Perhaps it's trying to make an escape under the fence. There could be so many reasons why the dog is digging.

Most dogs love playing and digging in the yard. This is because the soil there is usually softer compared to the harder-packed soil outside. This is especially true if you have recently tilled the soil for planting. Leaving the dog or puppy in a backyard for some exercise might turn into the pooch digging here and there as a way to burn up some excess energy.

A lot of the time, a dog will dig to relieve stress. It helps it get its pent up energy or frustration out and is a way for a dog to process their stress or anxiety. There is such a thing as canine nervousness. The tension triggers as well as the digging are a coping mechanism for the dog. However, it is a bad and destructive habit and it would be easier if it didn't happen.

You can do several things in order to deter a dog from destroying the yard. You could fence off any areas which might have been tilled recently, place some chicken wire over the top of your plant beds, go with your dog as he goes on these excursions and then pre-occupy him with something like a game, perhaps hide and seek or fetch.

There are certain breeds that are called earth dogs and these include Jack Russell, Carin, the Westie, and

Parsons. They tend to like hunting and exterminating vermin like groundhogs, moles, and voles. Dachshunds and terriers are specifically bred for chasing vermin and hunting. They will chase vermin into their holes and extract them.

Some dog breeds are genetically predisposed to hunting and killing critters, so if you think you might have any around it's a good idea to make sure your dog is walked using a leash.

For furrier dogs such as a Samoyed, Siberian Huskies, or Alaskan Malamutes, their heavy coats can be uncomfortable during the summer. They will dig holes in the ground where it is cooler and moist in order to get some relief from the heat. This can be counteracted by perhaps getting a big enough wading pool and filling it with just 3 or 4 inches of cool water. You could also keep those dogs inside with the air-conditioning on when it's really hot.

Is My Dog Digging For Fun?
Below are some steps for getting your dig-crazy dog to stop destroying your yard. It is actually not difficult to control the area the dog will dig. Your dog can have its own digging zone where the digging can be done without any harm to anyone.

Should you discover that your pet is one of those that are digging only for fun, you could allow a certain section of the yard to be his digging zone. The dog can enjoy itself and you don't need to sacrifice the entire backyard. Designate a specific area in the yard where the dog can dig to its heart's content and it knows it won't be reprimanded. A good portion area is around twice the dog's body length. Make this space obvious to the dog (and you) by placing some kind of visual border around it.

If you till the soil a little too it will make that space even more enticing to the dog. You might even bury some chewy toys or biscuits and let the dog have some fun digging them out. You can get down with him and dig as well, making it a game and a play experience for both of you.

You can make it a daily play and come up with a command for digging that the dog understands. Something as simple as "Go, Rover, dig!" Soon, he will start digging without being prompted, excited for what surprises he will find.

If your dog starts digging anywhere else besides the specified area, give it a sharp "NO!" then redirect him to the accepted location. This method mirrors the housebreaking techniques that puppy owner's use. Your dog will soon be drawn exclusively to the designated area for digging. He/she won't go anywhere else.

Don't feel too disheartened if your dog still digs in other areas of your yard. Just keep directing the dog back to its own digging area. At any time that you see him in the designated digging area try and reward him. This way he will keep going to that place whenever he needs to dig. You will find your yard hole-free after just a little while.

The Escape
Some of you may find that your dog is constantly trying to get out of your yard and may begin to wonder why this is happening. If you have a male dog that hasn't been neutered, it's probably because he wants to get to a female. If there are any female dogs nearby, it is likely the desire to get to them has triggered an escape attempt. Neutering your male dog can be the answer to this. Some dogs like Huskies, which are strong pack oriented animals, will try to get out of the yard and visit with other dogs. It's only natural.

What is the best approach if your dog is attempting to escape? Well, the pup is likely feeling lonely so a good idea is to not leave it by itself in the backyard. You could, if this is something you can do, get another puppy or dog. If this is not an option for you, perhaps doggie day care is something you could think about. Irish Setters and Huskies are particularly prone to loneliness and are friendly dog breeds.

If there is no doggie day care near you, or it's perhaps not affordable, you could consider a dog walker, or even a friend of yours who might be able to stay with the dog for a while during the daytime and keep it company.

Beagles, Bassett Hounds and other scent hounds are predisposed genetically to pick up on a scent and then follow it. It's hard to deny their natural inclination. Due to this, scent hounds really shouldn't be out in the yard alone without supervision. You could play a game, hiding some food or a food-carrying toy in your yard and allow the dog to find it. This will make the dog feel that the yard is an interesting place and the dog will not constantly feel the need to go elsewhere.

You also want to make an escape from the yard difficult for your pet. You might have to pour some cement below the fence line or reinforce the barriers by placing some heavy rocks up against the fence base. Perhaps some fence wire as well.

Digging out is but one escape route for dogs. Another is to go over the fence by either climbing or jumping. Check the fence height and your dog's height. Some dog breeds can jump quite high. You could extend the fence height using wire mesh. You could even try landscaping in a way to ensure the dog cannot do a run-up. For puppies who climb consider getting some fencing material which limits any foothold areas.

A dog will not climb a fence if he/she has been taught to respect barriers. This can be done starting with inside the home. A good starting point is a pet gate or baby gate. You can stand on one side and the dog on the other. You should reward the dog for standing or sitting nicely or for not actually touching the pet gate. If the puppy gets excited and puts its paws on the gate, just say "Get off!" or "No!"

Socializing a Dog with a Protective Nature
Let's say you're playing in the yard with your puppy or dog and the neighbor's ball comes over the fence. The boy next door shows up at the yard gate to get his ball back. Your dog rears up and begins to growl, leading you to believe that he might actually hurt the neighbor. The boy jumps back and you hurry to get to your dog as the boy runs back over to his house. In the dog's mind, the little boy fleeing has rewarded the

dog's protective behavior. He might even be waiting for a reward for a job well done.

Don't reward the dog because you will be rewarding it for chasing humans. This could, at some future date, get you embroiled in a lawsuit if your dog becomes overly aggressive and protective. It may even bite someone.

When a puppy starts discovering its environment, it will either advance boldly upon strangers or shrink in fear. It might start growling, barking, or even charging at people as it gets older. The dog is just behaving according to its nature, whether it is in fear or excitement. German shepherds, Rottweiler's, Japanese Akitas and Doberman pinschers have strong protective instincts that kick in when they are 8-18 months old.

In many other dog breeds, the protective instinct can be more out of fear than protectiveness. When dogs are fearful their tails hang low and their ears go back. They don't really like eye contact and see this as an act of aggression. They will usually lash out and try to bite what they see as their enemy. When a dog is fully in this protected mode, its tail will be raised high and its ears pointed forward. A dog that is fearful and sees no escape will bite and protect its territory.

Most people get a dog for company and lifestyle. Whatever the reason, you must act immediately to socialize your pet. Take him/her to dog parks, the pet store, other environments, and allow it to see all kinds of different people, and children especially. If your dog watches (on a leash and close to you) children playing, it will become familiar with their erratic playing movements and the sounds that are made when children play. It's a good idea to introduce your dog to children and the mail person.

Take your dog on as many excursions as possible. Have toys and treats with you. You'll be able to see how your dog reacts to different environments and you'll both learn things. The dog can learn what's appropriate and what's not in different situations. Your dog must learn that small people like your child should not be attacked.

Appropriate Yard Behavior
Community hotlines can be busy and are often used by people to complain about a dog that will not stop barking and is annoying others. You need to teach your dog or puppy to respect the space it has.

You must understand that when your dog barks it's trying to tell you something, to communicate. It might start barking loudly when strangers get close to your yard. The barking could intensify if a stranger challenges the dog somehow, and it feels threatened and needing to defend itself. Dogs might also bark if they smell something they think might be interesting or as part of their playing. Dogs might perhaps howl or bark if they are feeling lonely or isolated. It could be a way to call members of the pack, of which you are one.

When you've figured out what your dog wants to say with its excess barking, you must work out what is triggering the barking. If you're home in the daytime, keep a close eye on your dog so you can see what is triggering him/her. If you're not at home you might consider a webcam so you can see what's happening when you're not there.

The information that you discover should provide you with something to work with once you have an idea of what is setting the dog off. If, for example, you live close to a school, your puppy/dog may be barking more during the drop-off times and then again at pick up. It is a good idea to keep your dog indoors if you can during these times.

Of course, barking can also be something good that your dog does. For example, he/she might be barking to sound the alarm that a stranger is near the home.

The problem comes when a dog doesn't know when it's enough. About ten barks should be enough warning. If the dog continues to bark, thank him for the warning then command it to cease the barking. If it continues, command the dog to lie and stay. It should stop barking when it feels its chest in contact with the ground or floor.

If the dog cannot stop barking even after you've commanded it to lie down and stay, it might be necessary to get his attention using a surprise stimulus. This could be a sharp whistle or a water squirt on the nose. If this is what you have to do to guide your dog's behavior then it's important that your dog be kept inside during times when you're not at home.

An unchecked problem behavior like excessive barking will not go away but probably get much worse if the dog has more opportunities to engage in it. If this is the case, don't let the dog out into the yard without proper supervision. If just normal sights or sounds make your dog bark crazily then you might even consider a wall or fence that will limit the dog's vision. Remember to remind the dog to limit its warnings to ten barks, and then prompt it with "enough." After that, redirect or distract it with another behavior like "sit," or maybe "go to the mat."

When the dog obeys the command make sure to reward it using a favorite treat. A dog cannot bark while eating. It is also uncomfortable for a dog to continue barking if it is lying down. This is why you should use these commands for excessive barking.

You can eventually make your backyard a haven of security for both you and your pet. It just takes some commitment to training and some understanding as to why the dog is behaving in a certain way.

CHAPTER 6: HOW TO STOP INAPPROPRIATE CHEWING

Most people feel shocked and angry when they first see their dog destroying the furniture or their belongings. Try to avoid acting out in anger towards the dog and follow the below steps instead.

Try to work out why your puppy might be chewing on your things. Both younger and older dogs might start chewing on things as a way of fixing a problem they're experiencing. In order to correct the behavior you will have to work out exactly what the motivation is for the dog or pup to chew.

For puppies, the reason is usually comes down to teething issues. The chewing alleviates this pain. Puppies also chew sometimes as a way of exploring their surroundings, to get a stronger feel for the world around them. Puppies chew so they can learn what items are foods and what are not.

For dogs that are older, between 6 to 18 months, the chewing may be due to boredom. Sometimes this is why smaller puppies chew as well. When dogs are puppies and adolescents they have a lot of energy and if they don't get enough stimuli and are able to focus their energy, they will react by making their own kind of fun to entertain themselves. Usually, when a new dog is brought into a home, all the family will give it lots of attention, play with it, give it toys etc. Once the excitement wears off a little and a dog becomes just another family member, it can begin to feel a little lost without all the attention.

Another reason why dogs chew is because of spite or jealousy. Perhaps it feels displaced because a new pet or new baby has been brought into the home. Dogs may then lash out so they can try and get back some of the attention they were showered with originally.

Sometimes the new pet will get more time and attention. Perhaps your dog comes over as you're playing with your newest pet and begins chewing on the other pet's toy. In the dog's mind it is thinking, "If there's no toy this new one can't play."

Perhaps you're spending a lot of time studying and your dog starts to chew on your books. Perhaps you're away from the house a lot more often and the dog is alone. It might go for your shoes and chew on them. Because dogs are highly intelligent animals, they know what things you're choosing over them. Anything that a dog can see you choosing above it will become a casualty. The dog will do things to try and get some more attention from you and it really doesn't care if the books are from the library or your shoes cost $200. It is necessary and important for you to spend time with your dog, not only to save your belongings from being chewed into oblivion, but also to make sure your dog feels loved and a part of the family. Remember that dogs are pack animals not solitary animals and they need that company.

Something as simple as just 5 minutes of attention before sitting down to read or study, or before leaving the house will make it less likely that the dog will engage in any destructive chewing behavior. It will ensure your dog is in a better mood because it has received what it really craves – more personalized, focused attention.

What is the Dog's Problem?
Dogs are domesticated animals and have lived with humans harmoniously for many centuries. Dogs are seen as part of a family unit, and are expected to behave like it. This has led to dogs adopting certain human emotions and these include boredom, jealousy, spitefulness, neuroticism, hatefulness, and jealousy.

Just like human children, you will find that adolescent dogs have a hard time processing emotions and also controlling them. A dog's adolescent stage is usually between six to sixteen months. Just like humans, dogs will get better at handling their emotions once they've moved into adulthood. They will eventually learn to exercise greater restraint.

The Only Child Dog
The following story is true and happened to a couple. They got themselves a little puppy and doted on this cute little thing from the time it was placed on their arms. It literally went everywhere they went. They took him shopping and ran errands with his owners, even visited family and friends with them. It was so spoiled for love and attention and always walked proudly with its tail wagging wherever it went.

Then, something happened - his people came back home one day with a baby. Everything changed. The dog was left alone at home often, when the couple ran their errands he would be left in the car, and all the attention he was showered with wasn't there anymore.

On one occasion the couple came back after their errands and found that the inside of their car had been completely destroyed. Everything had been ripped to shreds – the carpets, car seats, padded dashboard, everything.

The dog was feeling rejected and lonely and became spiteful, resenting the fact that he now came second. The dog didn't hurt the baby because he loved it too but he also yearned for the good old days when he was number one. He didn't like being the dog. He wanted to be the focus of this couple's life. He lost his feeling of specialness and destroying the owner's car was a way of showing the couple how he was feeling. He was lashing out.

Redirecting a Dog's Chewing
Any time you catch a dog gnawing on something it shouldn't be, remove the object from the dog with a firm "No!" so he understands this particular item is not to be touched or played with. Replace the item with another object like an appropriate chew toy. This will distract the dog straight away from the other item that is off limits. He also won't feel so hurt that something was taken away from him if it is immediately replaced with something else.

Life changes are a part of life for everyone, including our pets. These changes can sometimes be quite challenging. Dogs are sensitive animals and will feel the changes. This may put them out for a little bit and they might engage in inappropriate behavior such as destructive chewing. That will be a good time to provide your dog with some extra tenderness and love as well as some extra training so as to prevent the behavior. Help the dog to adjust to any changes and remember that they are likely feeling anxious too.

CHAPTER 7: PROVIDING GUIDANCE TO YOUR DOG

Dogs are pack animals therefore they are social, just like their distant ancestors, wolves. Dogs will think in terms of teamwork and partnerships, the same way sports teams work together on a combined goal, which is to win. In order for a team to function well it will need structure, discipline, and respect. Your dog will actually look to you as well as the rest of the family as its pack. The dog relies on you all to help it survive, or as in teamwork, to "win."

Just like a successful, winning team, every member of the team (family) needs structure, discipline, and respect in order to function well and operate effectively in the pack. If these elements do not exist within the pack (family) chaos will ensue and the dog won't be able to tell who's in charge or who is supposed to be leading his team.

For dogs, leadership is a major factor. It gives dogs the security and sense of belonging they need. Dogs don't particularly care who the leader is; they just care that there is one so they can understand their role within their pack.

As a dog spends more time inside a home, it will start to clearly see what hierarchy exists there. It doesn't make any difference how many individuals live in the house; the dog will work out the hierarchy quite quickly. The dog will understand the structure of the household and that it is usually at the bottom of the hierarchy (unless there is another dog which is meeker). Dogs don't mind being at the bottom of the hierarchical ladder. As long as they know where they belong, they are happy.

It's the same with children. Kids who live in households without rules or boundaries will have some behavioral problems. This is due to the lack of rules, boundaries, and of course, leadership. The family leader has the responsibility of creating a set social order within the home. The leader must communicate this order so the dog understands it by watching the body language of the dog and making sure the dog is clear on who is the leader and in charge. A dog that doesn't recognize the leadership and order within a family will be a nightmare pet with bad behavior. It will be a problem for those around it.

It's not only the dog who must understand the order of his pack (or family) but the family members must also understand and follow the rules of how their dog must be treated. Ensuring every family member can come together and have the same clear understanding of the structure of the household is necessary. Respect is also necessary. Both understanding and respect from all members will ensure harmony is created and maintained between a family and their dog.

Resist Feeding Your Dog Outside of the Designated Times

Many dogs will beg for food or attention or both. In some cases, people see this as cute behavior and will encourage it. Unfortunately, doing this will create a whiny, annoying pet which visitors to the house will not be able to stand, not even for a short time. Most people see this for what it really is – bad manners. A dog that constantly hangs around and begs for food will quickly become annoying. It will become a top-notch whiner and will immediately whine the second it smells food.

Why is it Wrong to Beg for Food?

You must understand that when your dog begs he is actually demanding something. He is demanding it from you. The dog believes that it can wear you down using his begging and if this happens you will give it what it wants. Remember, dogs see the family as their pack. Anytime you surrender to the dog's begging, you're actually giving the dog some control within its pack. The dog should not have this control.

Some of you may think it's cute to see your dog lie on its back and beg for a belly rub. Perhaps you think it's also cute when the dog sits and stares at your food. Remember that begging is actually demanding in the dog's mind. Allowing this type of behavior can bring about some big problems later down the track, including the possibility for aggression on the dog's part.

How Aggressive is Your Dog?
It is easy to think that your dog will never get aggressive towards you because it loves you and you love it too. You might also not think it will become aggressive because it wants some of the food you have. It would be wise for you to reconsider this stance. It has happened. Let me tell you a story.

A friend had a dog and indulged it often, giving the dog a few bites of his food every time he would sit and eat. He would feed the dog some of his breakfast, his lunch, his dinner and his snacks. The dog began to grow and grow from a small puppy into an adult dog. Every time my friend gave the dog some food when it begged, he was actually reinforcing the dominant leadership position for his dog. One time, when this friend refused to give his dog some food, the dog cried and whined at first and then became aggressive barking and growling. My friend realized at that point what kind of a dangerous situation he had for himself. His dog suddenly jumped up at the table taking food off the plate, including some flesh from my friend's arm.

How to Eliminate Begging Behavior

Many of us could easily fool ourselves into believing that our sweet family dogs would never, ever hurt us in any way, even if they don't get what they want from us after begging. Perhaps you're thinking my friend's story above is extreme, but please don't do that. You must understand clearly that your dog continues with begging behavior because he has been rewarded for it in the past. A puppy must learn from the beginning that there are rules, you are the boss, and there will be no compromising on them.

It is a good idea to ensure your dog stays in an area far from the dinner table during mealtimes. It will take some effort and a little bit of time but the dog will learn that he/she must stay in that area until the meal is over. When your dog learns to do this, make sure you heap praise and attention on him and then reward him by giving him a nice meal – only after everyone has left the table after their own meal.

Why if Your Dog Growling?

Dogs growl because they find themselves in a situation that is uncomfortable. Many different reasons can trigger the growling. Your job is to observe the dog and work out what situations bother or annoy your dog. You then have the chance to train your dog so that it can tolerate the stimuli that it is reacting to.

It is often a human or animal approaching that could get the dog growling. The dog will growl if it feels threatened in any way. The growl is a warning to what the dog perceives as an intruder. It's a signal telling the intruder to back off. If the intruder retreats the dog will feel he's made his point and the growling will then stop. This then is canine communication in its basic form.

People need to understand these messages, especially children. When children approach a dog that is growling and they don't know to back off, the dog might then snap and try to bite the children if they continue to approach the animal.

Think About What You Would Do
What if your child goes towards your pet dog while the animal is lying down. The dog looks up and sees the child moving towards it. It then turns away and growls softly. Do you know what this means? Is the dog angry or upset with the child? What should you do in this situation?

Not all types of growling are bad. For the above situation the dog is actually trying to express to the child that it is not comfortable with him/her approaching and prefers to be left in peace. It's nothing personal.

Sometimes, dog owners will take this type of behavior personally. They might scold the dog or punish it for growling. Punishing a dog for instinctive behavior can then lead to bigger behavioral problems down the line. If you scold or punish a dog after it has tried to communicate with you in the only way it knows how – by growling, then you are actually stifling the dog's natural communication process. The dog might react more severely the next time.

Children must be taught about this type of canine communication. Whenever a dog starts growling at him/her it is imperative that he/she knows that the dog should be respected. The child should know to move away if this happens.

Make sure that your children know that they must stop whatever they're doing immediately if a dog begins to growl at them. Teach them to not run but to make eye contact with the dog while backing away slowly. Tell your children that they must tell you immediately what happened if they are ever in this situation. Then you can focus the training for the dog in a specific way so as to prevent this behavior from happening again.

CONCLUSION

After you have read a chapter or part that you need, take some action. Choose a technique that is outlined in the book and go from there. Keep in mind that training your dog isn't something that occurs overnight. It will take time and lots of patience. You and your pet will continue learning together and you can use this book to improve your knowledge.

Remember, training doesn't have to be difficult; it can be an enjoyable experience for both you and your dog.

THANKS FOR READING

We really hope you enjoyed this book. If you found this material helpful feel free to share it with friends. You can also help others find it by leaving a review where you purchased the book. Your feedback will help us continue to write books you love.

The Smart Reads library is growing by the day! Make sure and check out the other wonderful books in our catalog. We would love to hear which books are your favorite.

Visit:
www.smartreads.co/freebooks
to receive Smart Reads books for FREE

Check us out on Instagram:
www.instagram.com/smart_readers
@smart_readers

Don't forget your 2 FREE audiobooks.
Use this link www.audibletrial.com/Travis to claim your 2 FREE Books.

SMART READS ORIGINS

Smart Reads was born out of the desire to find the best information fast without having to wade through the sheer volume of fluff available online. Smart Reads combs through massive amounts of knowledge compiles the best into quick to read books on a variety of subjects.

We consider ourselves Smart Readers, not dummies. We know reading is smart. We're self taught. We like to learn a TON about a WIDE variety of topics. We have developed a love for books and we find intelligence attractive.

We found that each new topic we tried to learn about started with the challenge of finding the pieces of the puzzle that mattered most. It becomes a treasure hunt rather than an education.

Smart Reads wants to find the best of the best information for you. To condense it into a package that you can consume in an hour or less. So you can read more books about more topics in less time.

OUR MISSION

Smart Reads aims to accelerate the availability of useful information and will publish a high quality book on every major topic on amazon.

Smart Reads hopes to remove barriers to sharing by taking the copyright off everything we publish and donating it to the public domain. We hope other publishers and authors will follow our example.

Our goal is to donate $1,000,000 or more by 2020 to build over 2,000 schools by giving 5% of our net profit to Pencils of Promise.

We want to restore forests around the globe by planting a tree for every 10 physical books we sell and hope to plant over 100,000 trees by 2020.

Doesn't it feel good knowing that by educating yourself you are helping the world be a better place? We think so too...

Thanks for helping us help the world. You Smart Reader you...

Travis and the Smart Reads Team

WHY I STARTED SMART READS

Every time I wanted to learn about something new I'd have to buy 20 books on the topic and spend way too long sorting through them and reading them all until I arrived at the big picture. Until I had enough perspectives to know who was just guessing, who was uninformed and who had stumbled upon something remarkable.

I wished someone else could just go in and figure that out for me and tell me what matters. That's how smart reads was born. I want smart reads to be a company that does all that research up front. Sorts through all the content that is available on each topic and pulls out the most up to date complete understanding, then have people smarter than me package the best wisdom in an easy to understand way in the least amount of words possible.

For example, I got a new puppy so I wanted to learn about dog training. I bought 14 different books about dog training and by the time I got through the first 5 and finally started getting the big picture on the best way to train my puppy she had grown up into a dog.

Yeah she's well behaved. She doesn't poop in the house. I can get her to sit and come when I call. But what if someone else went in and read all those books for me, found the underlying themes and picked out the best information that would give me the big picture and get me right to the point. And I'd only have to read one book instead of 15.

That would be amazing. I would save time. And maybe my dog would be rolling over, cleaning up after my kids and doing the dishes by now. That my friend, is the reason I started smart reads. Because I wanted a company I can trust to deliver me the best information in an easy to understand way that I can digest in under an hour. Because dog training is one of many subjects I want to master.

The quicker I can learn a wide variety of topics the sooner that information can begin playing a role in shaping my future. And none of us knows how long that future will be. So why not do everything we can to make the best of it and consume a ton of knowledge. And I figured all the better if I can also make a positive difference in the world.

That's why we're also building schools, planting trees and challenging ideas about copyright's place in today's world. Because as a company we have to be doing everything we can to support the ecosystem that gives us all these beautiful places to read our books. Thanks for reading.

Travis

Customers Who Bought This Book Also Bought

Develop Self-Discipline: Daily Habit to Make Self Confidence and Will Power Automatic

How To Control Alcoholism: Proven Techniques to Stop Alcohol Abuse, Overcome Dependency, Break Addiction and Recover Your Life

Dealing With Anxiety: Modern Techniques for an Age Old Condition

Natural Ways of Boosting Testosterone: How to Bulk Up and Put Your Sex Drive in Overdrive

Minimalism: Declutter, Organize and Reclaim your Space

Unlimited Memory - Moonwalking with Einstein Steps to Photographic Memory

Unlocking Potential - Master the Laws of Leadership

Self-Esteem Supercharger: Build Self Worth and Find Your Inner Confidence